CW00517993

Bunny Girls

Bunny Girls

Angela Readman

Nine
Arches
Press

Bunny Girls
Angela Readman

ISBN: 978-1913437602
eISBN: 978-1913437619

Copyright © Angela Readman, 2022.

Cover artwork: 'Avgjørelsen / The Decision' © Katrine Kalleklev.
www.katrinekalleklev.no

All rights reserved. No part of this work may be reproduced, stored or transmitted in any form or by any means, graphic, electronic, recorded or mechanical, without the prior written permission of the publisher.

Angela Readman has asserted her right under Section 77 of the Copyright, Designs and Patents Act 1988 to be identified as the author of this work.

First published December 2022 by:

Nine Arches Press
Unit 14, Sir Frank Whittle Business Centre,
Great Central Way, Rugby.
CV21 3XH
United Kingdom

www.ninearchespress.com

Printed on recycled paper in the United Kingdom
by Imprint Digital.

Nine Arches Press is supported using public funding
by Arts Council England.

Supported using public funding by
ARTS COUNCIL
ENGLAND

Contents

'I made myself a doll's room in my cupboard.
It was curved and body shaped.
Inside it lived my doll,
busily writing.'

– Michèle Roberts

Christingle the Year Before
My Mother Called the Priest

They gave me the world when I was seven.
I carried it, a fat orange with a sputtering candle.

The sun would sizzle out if I spilled the wax.
I didn't get church, but I knew. Not to breathe

so hard. I must walk slow, set my world on the altar
with all the other worlds. Some looked squishy,

pinched to a pulp. Girls sucked Christingle juice
off their fingers, Brownie berets askew, bare swords

in their fruit. Nobody said what the wine gums meant,
but I held their stained glass until it burnt. I was sure

I shouldn't accidentally pop Jesus in my mouth,
but might. Later, maybe, with the lights out,

the flat chapeled by sleep. I sucked all the seasons.
Goldfinches, cardinals, the spurt and fall of trees.
I bit down into flickers, a leap in my teeth.

Pica

I ate all sorts when I was small. I could lick
a dish glazed, wolf afters and still wanted
more. There was space for something
not on my plate, a fizz of dandelion crazed
in the path. The Blackjack tarmac
of freshly dug roads made me salivate. I'd dip
bread in soup and taste gravel outside.
The burnt treacle of August in wait,
pavements sweating spilled slurpies
of kids flip-flopping home. Liquorice,
Twinkies, their hair flew high above bicycles
spinning a candyfloss sky. I sucked the peaches
of their voices, isolation dribbling down my chin.
The street looked wax when they left.
I peeled off a paper thin quiet, dropped
ribbons and gum. The road had only me,
sneaking out to inspect its scabs with a stick.
I got down, held the path in my hands
and sucked the sticky wounds to the bone.

K.I.S.S.I.N.G

I squirmed whenever I saw one coming, a kiss dropped off
the trembling tree the schoolyard sentenced us to.
I pulled up my hood, spit in my hair, the air zinging.
They happened like bluebottles, buried in pulled pigtails,
snapped jump-rope and bloody knees. I heard a buzz,
the anorak scratch of dark legs crawling into heads.
It was unclear when they'd become airborne, spat out
and blown. I saw body-popping larvae grow wings.
I stared at wet lips, fingers fond of nostrils, the snap
of kisses left our hands stringy as gum. Flailing,
my arms wafted puckers, a lasso slugging my face.
I swore they never hit me, but I know some did.
I tasted fingernails, jawbreakers, liver, and foil Virgin Marys
my mother told me would knock my baby teeth out.

Our Lady with the Sacred Heart

Our Lady drifts in after the party. The kitchen's a kilter
of stacked bowls, bottles reeling from being
the instrument that dared me to kiss seven boys.

She doesn't look how I think but moves the same.
Like water finding its level, lying still enough
to catch sky, cradle its blues. I know lasses

who get that look settling into lads' jackets, as if
folding bits of themselves, sighing out the spikes.
I am washing the dishes as if destroying evidence,

scraping myself away before my parents fly out
of Lanzarote. *I'm not Catholic,* I say, *I just sneak in
church sometimes if it's dreich. That's OK,* Mary says.

I'll call her that, though I don't ask. Just know,
the way I kissed Steven, Luke, knowing I wouldn't
if no one was looking. Lisa, Marie, Amy,

their laughs felt like holding baby chicks.
Mary picks up a dish towel, pours Quavers out
of a bowl and pops one. *I made you drop Baby Jesus*

in the school nativity, I admit, *I was six, I never
wanted to be you.* Mary shrugs, *Yeah, it happens.*
We're standing so close her cloth mices my wine glass.

I breathe almond oil, a river of hair dark as Lisa's
flowing into my shoulder. *I don't think it should be
called virgin if it feels this way,* I say. Mary nods,

her heart a pulsing light washing her gown pink.
The room blushes with it, a disco of roses.
Yeah, she says, *yeah I know.*

Bunny Girls

i.m Reuben Woolley

It's December, a small town up North skuttled
by twilight at 3pm. The street is a calendar of women
coming in after work, loaded with groceries
and turning on lamps. Sandra waits outside,

bunny ears biting her scalp, a plastic martini glass
glued to a tray in her hand. It's bitter, we flash
open coats to reveal our costumes – my Douglas Fir
dress boobed by baubles. Her fishnets and leotard.

I know nothing about mansions, only that we are six.
And that Bunny Girl tip-toes through the party, pinning
on her tail every five minutes. Boys pinching cotton,
fluff at her feet, silky bunny ears stroked so often
plastic stabs through the velvet like a fang.

And Sandra keeps laughing, picking wisps
of who we'll be all grown-up off the floor.
A lifetime later, someone tells me Hugh Hefner died
and that's all I see. Just some kid I used to know
with goose-bumps, a father picking up his son
joking if she was ten years older he'd fall in love.

I see my friend in streetlight unable to stop giggling,
wrapping her arms around that shiny bunny suit,
feeling for where it might be stapled on.

Peat

There stopped being brides in Manchester in 1989. Shops selling wedding dresses
went out of business. Florists wandered by canals. Bakers dropped their piping bags
wishing they cared about golf, given no choice but to take long weekends.

Unemployment, falling cinema attendance and The Problem with Wearing White
were considered factors on the news. No one knew. It was the year of Batdance,
house music and the bog man exhibit at the museum.

Visitors pressed their faces to glass cases, staring at the man preserved in peat.
He looked like he was sleeping, cradling the land. Leathery arms curved loosely
in front of him, as if allowing someone to slip in and out of an embrace.

They found he was in his twenties, yet he was ancient at the same time.
Girls clutched their satchels and wondered if they touched something
enough every quality it possessed would seep into their fingers.

Rent was increasing. Satin reminded too many people of rain, but
the most popular reason for not marrying was peat.
There was no arguing with it.

Women gazed at the camera and said *Some nights I think
about going clubbing but find myself laid in the garden semi-naked,
making angels in soil. Letting the cool soak into my legs.*

Angel Mechanics

My mother flung off her fur coat and left it,
a sleeping bear by the fire. We had to build an angel.
And it had to be now. That word, *angel*,
a breath mint sucked to lose its sharp angles,
she spoke it the way she called my name. *Angela,
Angela* a sliver of heaven in her mouth.

One palm swept the table, spilling ketchup, salt.
An unholy mess is what some things take.
Making an angel takes space. She chalked an outline
on laminate and ransacked the house, tipping
drawers, jugs full of pins, coins, foil strips of pills
to fill the angel with glints. *It won't do,* she said.

I flitted off to find knives, broken doll-feet,
milk lids and ribbons to give the angel skin.
We swirled on failed Airfix kits, nail polish,
glitter, a fritter of marriage certificate on the skirt.
A Lovehearts tin of my baby teeth hailed.
Laying a lock of hair, she once called sunshine

she could hold, my mother frowned. God,
we needed more. We had no wings. Just chicken
in the freezer & no feather in sight. We tore pillows,
shook out wild geese, a flock migrating to our glue.
We did it, she breathed, side by side we gazed
at our creation, down stuck to our hands.

Ode to Nosebleeds

I never knew when you'd show, you'd burst
in at weddings with rocket launchers, fling
Siamese fighting fish down my blouse.
I'd look down and see lines from stories
sprayed to my chest. Riding Hood,
pin pricks… you sewed poppies in snow.
Babysitters screamed for you, threw their pants
at your death metal. You flung battlefields at
their paper flowers, keys slithering down
my spine unfit to lock your hothouse
blooms. Fingers beaked, neck craned,
you poured skies down my throat. I'd follow you,
a map of echoes, discover the spotted quiet
of bathrooms, my personal cardinal absolving me
from loud parties. In a veiled space,
you rolled out a red carpet to show me
the watercolours I carried inside me,
my limited colour box billowing
into sinks, all my blushes broken loose.
It was like sketching animals in chiffon.
I often wished you'd stay a little longer,
drop the gun from my head, just keep on
painting all those horses swimming down.

Incomplete Autobiography in Blood Nouns

After Kathy Fish

An Honesty of Blood obeys store policy, snips the tags off dresses
worn once and denies my mother a chance to take anything back.

An Almanac of Blood is printed on my parents' bed, a honeymoon
conserved in sheets, pillowcases wax-wrapping dried roses.

A Constellation of Blood shoots across the frosted glass door
of childhood and leaves stars where my bruised father knocked.

A Companion of Blood is a dog walking me home, paws printing
flowers at my feet, a gingerbread trail to my friend's house.

An Intervention of Blood dives in front of me at discos, a bouncer
roaring *give the lady space* as my peers compare tongues.

A Tenderness of Blood lets my boyfriend in at sixteen, face a fist
unfolding into a picture of a baby seeing his mother kicked shy.

A Valentine of Blood never saw a rose it didn't like, scatters petals
on knuckles and tells me it knows the word *love* in twenty languages.

A Reassurance of Blood is a tongue licking underwear, an unsent text,
a violent man unforgiven, staying in pissing and smelling wild animals.

Nora

I spotted her before the others, the nurse in a glass
corridor, a bride of disgust dressed in white head to foot
other than a black bob, eyebrows skid-marks on frosty roads.
They didn't seem to belong to her. Nor her nails, so glossy
long, cherry-picking scalps to gather our thoughts.
I didn't want her to touch me, an acrylic rake so slow
I recalled my father dabbing spilled strawberry seed,
beads of my fear bedded under half-moons.
She must have been sixty. No ring on her finger
she spoke about weather, asked my name and I wept,
wouldn't crayon the gorilla, the gibbon either.
Girls gave one another plaits at story-time, stroked
blonde streams on the rug, dividing, dividing
I held in a scream. It was spring, light spun sequins
out of bowed heads, a pupae of dissected rainbows
atomed off us. The air suddenly looked alive.
I shut my eyes, small animal kingdoms in my lashes,
brows, foresting the down on my arms, legs, a torment.
I pictured invasions, a photo in the Sunday supplement
of a lady with a shaved head, so skinny her clavicles
and sternum were horned beetles squatting on her chest.
But instead of her face hung over a loose uniform,
I glued on my own. Stripped of ribbons, pearly slides,
studded in follicles bare as disobedient dolls, dreams
sieved to full stops. I didn't know about oils
or steel combs, if anyone told me I'd never believe it.
I'd seen more. I saw myself as a ghost hovering
behind all this laughter, cats' cradles and knock-knock,
the toll of the daily bell pelting us at the sun.

The Female Alien's Dictionary

after Craig Raine

School is a storage facility for animal songs and wobbly teeth.
Class photos are assessments of the progress of smiles graded 1-10.
A photographer is an alien with amnesia, he waves to understand birds.
Mittens are sleeping bags to give rainy roses and railings a rest.
An umbrella is a manual for turning inside out. Skipping rope
is a bridle for the invisible horses you ride through traffic.
A playground is a concrete boardgame without instructions.
The painted hopscotch is yellow doubting the value of existence.
The alphabet is a song wiring *I am here* all through your body.
A can only be for *apple,* not *axolotl* or *anus* leaping off dictionaries.
A dictionary is a recipe for a million lives, bubble-gum, war and soil.
Spelling matricide at a christening is the same as dropping a baby.
Television is an aquarium where mermaids live. Brightness
is a dial to stop you detonating. Nipples are buttons boys use
to change the atmosphere. A vest is a duster that remembers
paddling pools and monkey's blood. A bra is a girl pretending
to be a fly and failing most of the time. Knickers are calendars.
The speaking clock is a hotline home, a siren screaming
from the UFOs that land in your hair.

Truth & Lies from a Spectrum Childhood

1. It's crucial to smile for photos, nobody will tell you which type of cheese.
2. Storytime is an orange carpet. If you inch onto cool tiles under the table, Goldilocks spits out her porridge and Kodiaks rip her to shreds.
3. Fluorescent is easy to spell, all day it will try to scream how.
4. Hands can be cradles and locks. Holding Halloween lanterns, you're a baby in utero.
5. Baby dolls will be judged if they wear hot pants. Girls will be if they do not.
6. Flashing your pants is a logical way to discover the day of the week.
7. Ms Calendar loves to be serenaded whenever you sign the late register.
8. The sparkly shirt in your mother's wardrobe is a panther dying in a jungle.
9. If you lie inside after school, the day slims to a strip clear as cheese singles. It will peel off you if you close the door, the hush of suede shoes rubs off.
10. Velvet cushions are pets that don't bite, stroking you can tell if they might.
11. Hamsters need sleep and apples.
12. Apples are green. They grow in people's eyes. Bite in to see the air write *bruise.*
13. Bruises are sunshine caught in your skin, under clouds other weather's developing.
14. Autumn is knitting with holes in. Spring is where winter washes its hands. Summer is. Sunsets are jeans and T-shirts running in the wash.
15. The ambition of dresses is to match the wallpaper.
16. Walls are rivers waiting to happen.
17. The rain in the gutter illuminating the ceiling has more to say than your teacher.
18. *Look at me when I'm talking to you* means losing your shadow, a sapling shooting from a varnished floor and up through the window.

Girly

Maybe it's because I wore nothing but gingham until I was eleven. Or, because I'd still grind with my girlfriends in hot pants and bralettes, like a Pollyanna gone feral. Maybe it's because all my baby teeth dropped out at six. I kissed *everyone*. Or it's the jawbreakers I licked until red painted my lips with the lipstick I wasn't allowed. Or it's because our curtains stayed closed a whole summer. Maybe it's because I snuck out and stole the orange juice next door. Maybe it's because my sister's shoe looked lonely, a lovely kitten heel. Maybe it's because she was Supergirl every chance she got. Maybe she was prettier than she knew, and some people feel too alive to be afraid of walking alone. Maybe a smile isn't always a smile. Maybe it's because my mother froze when a zombie cheerleader knocked at our door. Or it's how I shepherded her inside, arm around shoulder, my Lisa Simpson cheek making her jaundiced. Maybe it's because having your birthday on Halloween sounds the bomb until you realise all your cakes will be coffins. Maybe it's because biology killed me. And I hated sitting next to that kid who kept drawing anatomically correct vaginas on his notebook. Or it's because I got my period once in gymnastics. Maybe it's cruel all shorts aren't black. Maybe he heard about that and felt sort of sad. Maybe because his mother left, and the house got so lousy some kid pinned him down and wrote UNCLEAN on his forehead. Maybe magic markers are everything that is wrong with society. Maybe it's because he's only 5ft 4 and no one else said yes. Or because when I look in the mirror, I still see gingham. Maybe I can't stand looking like an outline on pavement. Maybe I watch too much Disney, and when they brought that shoe from the street where my sister was last seen, for a second, I thought Cinderella. Maybe I'm a sucker for bottled beer and whispering who I'd fuck, kill or marry under a moon like Fanta. Maybe it just felt right, like someone froze the documentary forever playing in my head. Maybe it was dumb, and I don't care. I let him, let myself. Ever since I've been stroking my belly whispering *Girly, Girl…*

I Told GI Joe Thanks for Nothing

I showed GI Joe the Sindy house. He didn't fit,
the lift swung off its runners. I showed him
the dining room, silver knives, spoons.
He showed me his rubber fists gripped a gun.
I carried him to the bedroom, a monogrammed suite,
showed how easy the gold-leaf rubbed off on my pinkie.
I pulled off his boots and witnessed his AWOL foot,
but he couldn't get in bed straight away. Oh,
I told him that. This was Sindy's place, right?
He had to be sweet first, needed to tell her about love.
Joe made me pull the string in his spine, instructed me
to Hold Fire. I peeled off his clothes, stroked a scuffed knee,
the turtle he must keep in his plastic pants.
What about butterflies? What about flowers?
I asked where he kept all his gifts, he told me
his stomach wasn't moulded like that. Look
right, left, he'd stare straight ahead if I nudged
the scab on his scalp. Sindy wore a baby-doll nightie
and floated towards him. See how pretty? I said.
He said he knew it, but no, he couldn't tell her.
I lay her on the duvet, legs spread, arms raised,
her whole body a star shining for him. Kiss, I said.
I put his hand on a breast but he wouldn't hold it.
He wanted to know where the cord in her neck
was that let her say yes, yes, oh God, yes.

Miss Monroe's Body Double on the Set
of *Something's Got to Give*

One August, I was the shadow of a star. I walked and guys angled lamps.
I switched a light on under my skin, saw photos of you skinny-dipping
and dived into that pool. My shadow was you. I slipped out of myself
into its silk. I breathed out and people thought of you.

I'd been dating a mechanic for years, but something clicked. I held
his interest in your pearl fist. Men lit my cigarette, fingers silvered
by grazing your breasts in newsprint. So many small stones stitched
to gauze blinking like hail on freshly washed clothes.

I accepted every soda I was offered, brushed a cameraman's fingers
and wondered if a president's feel the same. Some days I pretended
my cola was champagne, a zillion meteors in my mouth. Others, I knew
you imagined champagne was milkshake cooling gasping lips.

That summer, I felt it too, a sort of burning, black holes in my stomach.
Someone would mistake me for you and I'd feel the weight of people
waiting for me to laugh a smile onto their face.

I was a woman walking into her house discovering the dog she left
drooled for her scent. I was a figure at a poolside seeing her babies
learn to swim. At night, I strolled platinum streets in the wig,

a snowstorm balanced on my skull. I saw my silhouette adorn bus stops,
bars, a trophy awarded to disappointed men. They flicked through me,
a calendar of dreams, so long as I didn't turn around.

Ode to a Severed Head

I found you digging. Buried
in a jungle of rocket, a porcelain head,
like a dropped snowdrop bulb. No sign
of a body. I lifted you wanting
the sun to wash through you
as a Sunday might worship a china cup,
show me the possibilities of bone.
You would have none of it. Skull
stuffed with clay, I ran you under
the hose, wiped clarts off your face,
a clenched bud of lady. Lips, cheek,
blushes worn grazed, a strand of bronze
paint clung to your curls. I wanted
it to be clear who you had been. See it
in your chin, a shepherdess lilt
or milkmaid nod that needed no churn,
arms or legs to be completely herself.
But, no, all you were is a head,
a clean-cut filling the yard
with clasped hands, dancing girls.

When the Body Refuses to be a Temple

I found my body was a flat. I put up silk curtains
but passers-by could see my walls were bare. I decorated,
bought lovely furniture but nobody wanted to live there.
I built skyward, made my roof glass.

I found my body was a mansion. I rattled around it,
bumping into mirrors. Dancers raved through
in terrible trainers, drank me dry and soiled my couch.
I installed locks and window shutters.

I found my body was a prison. I couldn't see out.
It spoke only echoes and sang ballads about how lush
it once was. And yet something moved in for a day,
I felt it fall down the stairs and dig a tunnel.

I found my body was a church. I lay on its altar
offering its prayer to anyone who wanted to come in.
The confessions of strangers wore limestone, smashed
stained-glass saints. I axed the doors.

I found my body was a Wendy-house. I polished
cups and set plates with daisies, but couldn't move.
The dolls picnicked on my despair, I let them
sip air and slipped under the floor.

I found my body was a shed. I saw my coat
on the hook when I walked in, a nest of blue tits
lining my pockets. I sat, closed my eyes and I slept.

Another Miss Universe

That night we crashed the pageant, none of us beauties,
no winners in the family. We stormed the ballroom,
lights spinning galaxies, the red velvet rope
of everything our mothers told us sawn off our ankles.

The lovely surrounded us, a bloom of blonde, faces
open as glasshouse flowers, judges holding up scores
of how easy they'd be to love. Miss Brighton, Bristol,
Miss this, Miss that, the wonderful swirled their talent.

We held another baton, the homely who won't stay home.
Ordinary, plain, we rushed the stage. Twirled, not
to show our best sides, just what was. Tiger stripes
of our bellies, the pearls pocked to our arms.

The lipsticked mouths of scars took bites out of perfection.
True, we quivered like horses, lips drawn over teeth released,
awkward smiles set free. Here we are, we said, unpretty, alive.

In a lottery ticket tickertape we accepted dandelions
graceful as bouquets of lilies. That night we took it all,
the laughter, the gasps. We bowed to the tears
glued to our plastic crowns.

Letter to a Twelve-Year-Old Self

Lass, I've built you a cottage so far from here,
the lamp in your room is a lost orange stamp.
Nights like this are postcards that needn't arrive.

It doesn't look like much, but I've shook silverfish
off the rug and welded a bulletproof roof.
I've planted roses, peony, a bed full of lipsticks

you can nick if you like. I've sprinkled skirts
on the floor of your room, let the carpet
grow wild. Come, wander into my garden,

last night's rain licking the compasses of your legs.
It's all ours, lass. The fridge jammed with jelly, pomegranates,
pins. Come, sit, eat. I've painted deer on your dish.

Look out tonight, through the blackhole
of mouths sucking the lights out of the house,
telling you, telling you why you're no good.

Look, dip your fingers in frogspawn, stroke
my jade pond. When your mother burns your stuff
on the lawn, pick the daisies and chain yourself to it.

The Usherette's Eczema

It allowed her to picture lizards escaping the zoo, stepping
into the cinema for the first time. Darkness was her natural habit.
Uniform crisp, hat a sinking yacht, the usherette loved her job.

It was to be stone when a film began. Not a shuffle or wince
at a machinegun or bomb, shiver or jump. At the end of the aisle
she gave herself to dust flocking to the screen. Felt herself fade
as couples lock lips and shy palms found knees. Cigarettes
laid on a tray with a bricklayer's hand, she stroked
boxed fruit gums like a woman in love.

Sometimes, she caught a glance. Men admiring her lofty legs,
a flash of lightning onscreen. The scene cut to night, dimmed
the flare of her arms, a mosaic, knuckles to scalp. Here,
she considered buying a crocodile purse, tortoiseshell compact
like everyone else. Scratching, flakes of skin rose to light,
she gave birth to moths.

For a second, she understood the very short man sitting
on his stool in the box-office, flirting from the matinee
to the late show. He kept his window so clean it looked
like a postcard from another version of himself.

Flass

Always thought there was another lass
in me somewhere, a sweetie buried
beneath the sour plums, pear drops
I sucked to stop myself swearing.
Off we went to the dentists
before the dance, my doppelganger
mounting the leather first.
Mouth wide, legs crossed,
black Mary-Janes pointing
at a man and a penguin mobile.
I sat in a plastic chair waiting.
The flass of the pump filling
a spitting image of my fifteen-year mouth
with fjords, steel scraping plaque
to unearth a laugh like flying fish
caught by finger shielding lips.
See, isn't that better? Show me that smile.
I saw my other-self climb down fawn footed,
the mirror a headlight roaring
towards to my face. My doppelganger
flashed a smile as instructed. It looked
like someone driving a van with gears
they can't handle. I felt it roar towards me
climbing in the seat, a saddle still warm.

A Bluebottle Summer

I don't cut the liver but slip it in my pocket and slide
out of lunch, meat juice leaking through my blouse.
I fling it on the grass, the dog I imagine wolfing it vanished,
a bluebottle sunning itself on blood.

In an alcove facing a dumpster, knees tucked
to neck, my skydiver jump. I stroke my smocked leg,
the iron embroidery of a scab. I didn't swallow apricot stones
like my cousin. My stomach aches without anyone saying
leaves must be uncurling inside me, but I know I grow bark.

I nudge the crisp lip, fingertip tracing the colour of orchids,
peeling skin I flower bright as the Valentine's drawn
for my mother, a suck of felt pen to keep a lonely heart red.
It's like licking batteries, my tongue vampired by rust
until I rip off the scab whole and swallow it. Charged.

The Black Egg

I was always afraid of silence.
It was a sinkhole in my mothers' house,
a swirling flood beside her bed.

I walked around it like a black egg,
felt it crackle. Something unfeathered
and starving inside it, pecking

a burrow out. It would swallow me
if I didn't bang spoons on pans.
Bark, roar. Howl about stars,

blue moons, funky towns,
country roads, Jolene
and chickens. Girls and boys

banded love about the radio,
couples discoed, squeezed, held hands.
I knew it was to stop themselves

falling into all that silence,
a frozen lake full of piranhas
and iron bedsteads
creaking under their shoes.

Man Dusting

My husband has been asleep for so long
I no longer pick the mushrooms that grow
between his legs. I dust around the bed,
nightgown brushing the mat, a moustache
of dust gathered on the hem.

I've become a ringmaster of spiders. I study
the marquees on his face, make cobwebs
a mirror of my breath. Since love went to sleep,
winters have laid in my hair, summers rolled over
and grilled toast flecks on my hands.

Whilst he has aged like an unread book, his lips
un-dogeared by smiles. Those thoughts
we all return to fail to underline his brow.

I bow to his dreams with a soft cloth, floorboards
cursing my feet. I just can't tiptoe anymore.
I've stopped oiling groans off the doors
and shushing birds in the eaves.

The swallows dip in/out of his mouth all July.
They do this each year. Whenever I miss hearing
someone whisper my name, I fling
the windows wide open and let everything in.

Ode to a Dust Sheet

You have been a still from *Fargo* on our bed.
Snow laid so crisp we were afraid to jump in, roll
the steam of our arms and legs across your plain.
Cotton taught us ourselves, sketched the grey haloes
of sleep, knives of feet, the mushroom spill
of damp summer nights. Winters freckled you
in cocoa, Nutella, you hold the birthmarks
of the babies we dreamed of, all our dark
constellations of blood. Filthy now, your ruin
all this life. We bow to your flatlines, so little
untouched, slips folded beneath by us dazzling
packet white. We are sorry for the rest, stains'
inexplicable fog, days sifted out of our skin,
a dust we unknowingly showered you in.
We lay you to rest, sheet, on this couch,
sacrament thin, speckled in gloss,
a duck egg hatching a fresh room.

Hush

Fuming, I storm out of the kitchen and the quiet
introduces itself. The swallows vanish, a barn owl
arcs beneath contrails, soft as a compress on a graze.

My husband isn't far behind, stepping outside,
dustpan of ash rising, a blizzard rewound. I point
up, along. No gasp, but the ryegrass swaying hush.

Dusk pulls apart to reveal a pale satin lining,
a flashlight of feather on stonewalled cloud.
I thought I knew what silence is.

All day, we've dragged a hush through the house,
jammed it in our mouths. We have fought
over nothing that is everything, lips bolted doors
with jangling keys chained to pride.

And here, a soundless now dropped upon us.
The owl plots the boundaries of hawthorn
in chalk, wings hammering a hundred shutters
to the mouse-glutted hedge.

I stand with my husband, stare at the soar
lifting whatever was so important out of our heads.
Our fingers reach at the dip, clutch this business
of living by so many small deaths.

Psalm for a Street Swept by Plague

Let's lower our eyes to deserted roads, dandelions
growing through doormats. Let's press our hands
to silence, hedgehogs asleep in bonfires unlit. Call it
a prescription for air, a wedding to dust, a test
for a pregnant pause. A kit for fixing tyres slashed
by stillness, a clock wound to now, a pulse wired
to midnight, a heart never opened. Or closed.
Make it a toast, if you like, raised with sea fret.
Beer seething in kegs, the spirit of an untold joke
lifting a bubble-wrapped clink. Make it a mass
for fist fights, drunk taxi ranks, kebabs never slipped on,
an unfractured skull. Just make all this nothing
a prayer of birds. Deer driving their faces
through the wings of parked cars, a rain-dance of hoof.
It seems we should kiss something, so let's.
Kiss the words never spoken, babies unborn,
a goodbye to the doors nailed shut in our chests
whenever we pretend to know.

Commercial for the Uninvention of Bread

This is not just your hunger. This is gazing into fridges
spreading cheese on your knuckles, the disappearance
of one Easter you ate outside in shorts. It's a portrait
of your mother slicing her disappointment in half.

This is kneading clouds in a bowl, afraid a slammed door
will ruin the rise. It's wobbling in at 3am, sawing crusts
of Is this it? It's smearing Marmite on baby's cheeks,
weekdays sealed in plastic pyramids, air unwrapped

at your desk, biting in. This is your wander around
supermarkets squeezing man after man to find something fresh.
It's the thought hotdogs all look like they forgot a dirty joke.

This is a B&B built in Frosties, sunshine staining
your shirt, the queen of hearts dipped in soup, a night stop
at service stations scraping a thought of where passers-by go.

This is your lack, a picnic of grit, this is closest you will ever get
to swans. It's a ritual of ordinary dissolved, a knife carving
a minute of silence into morning. This is the toast you forgot
how to make to everyone you've ever known.

The Survivalist's Guide to Love

After, we were still searching but dating had changed. Our ads
made love sound like an island someone might get stranded on.

*I have fishfingers, but no bread…There are eggs in my fridge I've painted with
fangs…I don't know if I'm a good lover, but I can make a pine pew into a bed
and a bed into a wilderness.*

It was so long since we touched, since we dared, we were bunnies
quivering into the world. Our selfies had faded to dots, all we had
were snaps of useful hands.

*Here is a picture of a kitten I sewed…This is my loaf, it's not pretty but it
rose…OK, I can't paint, but I know how to describe a beach so blue you could
surf…The butterfly here needed sugar, I carried it a mile in my hands.*

It felt deafening to big ourself up like we used to; we had seen just how
small we are. We all had so little we carried our flaws like bouquets.

*I can't swim, but I can hold my breath for five minutes…Seahorses make me
sad, ever since I read they're the ghosts of drowned foals…I have a guitar I keep
leant against a wall, it hums to my footsteps. This is all I can play.*

It was a struggle to slip off our distance, the long days alone wrapped
us in other arms. Late at night, we stayed up flashing messages, an SOS
of ourselves.

*I won't kiss you, but I can tell you how it feels. Looking at a sunset without a
phone, slipping on a red dress with a rip, catching the starling that flew into
your house, taking it outside and watching it rise.*

Bringing Back the Day

It wasn't flash, a slackered June afternoon,
yet we wanted it. The grass shrewd with stones,
drizzle steaming our jeans, knuckled light.

We got up, dusted pepper off our fingers
and set about bringing the day home.
I wound in a stream, snipped swallows off lines.

You bundled a rape field into the car
and the wind switched off its lamp. Holding
one end, you another, we rolled a wild verge,

ripped nettles in perforated strips.
Crows drifted over, scorching their shadows
into each other, we grabbed those wings

the way we hadn't quite kissed. The sun
was a lemon cord; I tugged once. It was light.
It all packed so small we forgot about it until April,

when there was no choice but to drag the day out,
drape it throughout the house. Floors crawled,
wallpaper finched, flicked us sparrows.

I called your name and dog roses uncurled.
The sky was a balloon rising over the bed.
We lifted both hands and held on.

Alternative Endings for Hitchcock's *The Birds*

Or we learn to live with more birds. Hang
galvanised clotheslines, wrecking-ball feeders.

The school children don't run, but learn
Raven, a salty liquorice tongue adults
snap in their mouths. Girls make way

for crows on the swings. Raise orphan
fledglings, bones and dead mice dangling
off lips. Boys kiss magpies called Darling.

The lovebirds fly free and, of course,
have sex with everything. The blue tits blush
a red streak. Bodega Bay is painted white.

The blonde marries but can't forget birds.
The gifts jackdaws leave on her doorstep,
shiny keys, seashells, slick Lego hands.

It's morning, she flips bacon without eggs,
axes her kitchen window and spreads fat
on the table. Sparrows wing in, gulls, terns,

pink-footed geese. The screen zooms in
on the flock, the sky is a dust cloth
shaking out her whole life.

How to Make a Blackbird

Take the wire off the fence to build bones,
spring a foot, flint a tail. The legs are harder
than you think. Grab a pillow and tear, poke
in falling silt, frozen puddles and pinpricks,
a dab of blood heart. Now, you are ready
for black, a hundred or so. Unroll the wool batt,
pull wisps of smoke off the dogs, slug trails
off storms, and stab. There's no sweet way
to do this, needle with burrs. The steel bite
of chest will fork your fingers. It may take years;
work after midnight for feathers. Felt in fuming fires.
A strap of funeral shoes, bra-hook claws, before
looking at the eyes. Take sunlight, the flash
of every gold ring you lost and never bought.
Sink it all in, fill the spaces with oil splashes
and rain. Listen to Norwegian Wood,
Morning has Broken, knife the song
to your throat and sing.

Curator of Rain

I attend my doorstep for the slug smackdown. Salt Stain,
Puddle-gob, Jizzsock, Swirling Cleaner of Algae gluing
orgies to the window. Lino Sailor, Shell Shedder,
Architect of Pots, Ice Clot, Tar Bolt, Nagging Reminder
the Wise Should Wear Shoes, even indoors. Brushing
the surface won't do, not for you, nothing satisfies
but the fat ooze, Houdini of Nooks, Spy of Barefoot,
Professor of Shiver and Squelch. Jellied River, Creeping Bruise,
Shifter of Dirty Lace decorating the world with fake glitter.
Blackbird Big Mac, I see you, Curator of Rain, a mantel
of storms, cleaner of crops, muscler of walls. Just me, you
& you, you, Slug, your snotwork a scribbler of notes
to insomniacs and shut-ins, Slug, silversmith of night.

10:58am in November

Morning slips into my room carrying orchids.
The walls are bare, papered for a moment
by shadow, tendrils sprung through a grey cage.

I can't touch the window for the radiator, desk.
It opens itself to me like a palm full of prayer.
See the fence? it says, the snowberry? This

feeder, swinging with the ghosts of possible birds?
It is not a large pane, only a series of small ones.
The day hangs itself in chipped frames,

the view prairied, a bit here, there. Grass,
wall, sky, fence, a wave of ducks passing
their hunger from one glass to the next.

Morning peers over their shifting boulder to say
See, isn't this worth giving praise? Getting dressed?
I don't answer, before she's on her way,

flicking through next-door's gate, she builds
a steeple, makes a church of the red vase
on the ledge and sets it on fire.

Haugh

Haugh, a strike of the match, flame snatching logs.
Haugh, the wind breathing down stove pipes,
slates bucked, the flight of the trampoline,
barrel rolled, the compost spilling slick guts.
Haugh, the orange kite like koi carp, a kid
reeling in his piece of sky, the pull and snap.
Haugh, a flap of tarp, a fisherman fixing his boat,
the boatyard's alley a thief swiping scarves.
Haugh, the wing beat of geese, a crashed wave.
cormorants flashing sand, upturned umbrellas,
a cough of an old man walking a dog past the pub.
Haugh, the bark, fox screech, owl swoop,
crows pouring out stillness flicking oil at stone.
Haugh, the fallen branch, oak in the road,
the dying engine, caught breath, a woman panting
uphill delivering eggs, an awareness of the crack
of all things in her fingers, lodged against her ribs.

Arrival of the Siberian Swan

The afternoon is a landing with a fused light.
The swan pours into the lake and a fisherman
recalls his first wife drawing skin off the milk.

It can't be here yet. Summer hasn't quite rusted
through, amber leaves hang, sunlight breaches
branches like lemon cotton snagged in a door.

And yet, it is here, ripping stillness off the water.
The bird's smog-dipped neck, dirty blonde
as a beard, a web of pipe-smoke and frost.

The swan glides close and out of nowhere
the fisherman sees his mother's fingers gluing
a smashed tail to a porcelain bird when he was young.

There should be a warning memory acts like this.
That in a wave of water folding itself
he'd recall how women he used to love moved.

Jacket lifted, the fisherman flaps. It's October.
Where one swan is, soon a hundred will sail, carting
in winter feather by feather, laying it on his house.

Hissing, he chases the short days out of sight.
Above him, a swan soars with the sound
of an orchestra announcing it hasn't arrived.

The Blow Torch

Turned up in a sack of screws and string,
the blow torch, liver-spotted with rust. That flash

of brass in his father's shed caught him, a candle
spitting out the dark. It was ours now.

Who knew where to get paraffin? Anything
about pumps, the virtue of not using a gun.

I placed it in a pot of vinegar, scoured the shaft
with steel wool. The sunshine of Sundays

knelt in its belly, flashed fringes of a small boy
looking up, watching the season's fat curl fall

from stripped windows, frames blonde for an hour.
I handed my husband the torch in silence.

He cut the cord off a lamp and wired in a bulb.
I stood beside him in our lounge, staring

at the lamp. For a fleck of forever I stood like that,
burning to ask if we dared switch it on.

The Still of Churches

Just me and someone else's father sit alone
in a church. He flickers to a candle, lights it
and stares at the bone steeple of his hands.

I look away. I'm aware of outside. The roof
counting a rosary of rain, a blue tide of stained
glass dragging out the last of the afternoon.

The deer strides in at the side of the altar,
cocksure as my old man, as glassy eyed. Its hooves
cathedrals of dirt, insects and stomped leaf.

It has no right be here, a deer sniffing echoes
of prayer, carrying a chandelier of rain, antlers
burnished by the candle I lit believing
in nothing but the still of churches.

I look up with the stranger, hooked by the stag
striding out, steam rising off flanks. Our eyes lock
fixed on a door ajar, a silver purling of breath
decorating our losses. Hanging strings in the air.

After Fifteen Days I Leave the House

It has rained and leaves torch the path.
While I slept, October snuck up and washed
the last of summer's things.

The morning is an aired room, orange
scraps scattered on beds, the sage pot
rolled on its side. I pad across grass,

slippers dark tongues lapping milk, a bone
of sunlight laying a finger on frost.
It is not my shadow, surely? Breathing

a broth of fallen apples, burying sunflowers'
clocks of burnt afternoons. It can't be,
but it is me, dyeing the grass cardigan,

toadstools umbrellaed by poncho. I walk
and the tarp draped on builder's sand dresses
me in a ballgown. But how will I dance now?

I think it starts with a bow to stones in rain,
slates kicked off the shed, this wasps' nest dropped
by a bench, all its dirty lace still intact.

H_2O

That week at Alnmouth I become water.
Kids sailing tyres, women screaming *Be Careful,*
a tongue in my ear. I soaked it all in. I gathered
the spit of skimmed stones, the look on your face,
and was vapour. I fell in a hot shower hours later,
you opened your mouth, deblonded.
I did this once as a kid, a print of salmon
leaping on assembly curtains. Goldfishing
Jerusalem, Ms Dunn said I had a sweet voice
and I was airborne, fat with puddled wellies,
milk glasses, soggy cardboard and spitballs.
With you, I rose to be one with breath,
bathroom fans, boiling kettles, spilled wine.
I was a rolling skin pelting myself
at your body in beads to restring.
You bathed in my leglessness, draped it
on radiators, dived for small fish. I rose,
lashed the estuary and saw swans swim
where my mouth used to be. That last night
with you something sunk in, built a dam.
I stopped knowing how to flow into your arms.
I was a cloud in a mirror wiped into a face by a cuff.
I left you drop by drop, sipping a glass of rain.

How to Get with the Invisible Woman

Switch off the music and listen to the soft rock of your life,
something mouthing lines from forgotten romcoms.
The invisible woman wants you again.

Buy flowers on forecourts, neck drizzle-licked, the scent
of petrol and laundry walking you home. Let the wind
counting leaves be a woman laughing or summer

whispering *at last*. Linger beside exits, hold shop doors
for weeks, the best sex of your life or fog walking through.
Look in the mirror and ask, are you behind me?

Don't be afraid to lean for a kiss. And miss. Kiss
kitchen cabinets, fridges. Be known to go all the way
with trees, a scorching breath in your ear, weather or foreplay.

Check into cheap hotels and wander about crushing on objects,
each chair a lap dance, bed a spooned hip, if you could only sit
right. An unseen company will straddle you.

You'll learn silence so well you could speak goldfish,
understand the sound a moth makes breaking into its wings.
You may doubt she's out there, stand still and turn,

arms empty to feel her. That woman barely there, bones
larches mid-flight. Hold on loosely, know she can
disappear any second, all it takes is a step back.

Procedures for the Detective after Thelma & Louise

You can't stand above that canyon forever. The freeze-frame dissolves to slush, you want to hold those ~~girls~~ women in sunglasses flying forever. You want to see sky, sky, sky, sky like four movie nights in their eyes. You can't. Don't look down.

Listen to your colleagues at the station. Whenever some ditz dies there's paperwork. Damn waste of a classic car. The cowboy who stole Thelma's cash is on bail again. Keep thinking of the gestures he made halfway out the door, grinding an invisible girl.

You will want to buy flowers coming home, can't say why. Your wife sniffs with suspicion or gratitude. Be unsure. Think of that husband whose wife revved herself at the clouds scraping pizza off his shoe. Attend the sink after supper, wash the plates. You can do more.

Drive by the dead woman's place again. Look through the windows, the room as she left it. Embroidered roses on the dishcloth. Lace curtains flinging butterflies at the parched golf course. Slot your Visa in the door, sit in a woman's house for a while.

Look at the photo of that girl with the baton. That twirler she was, all skinny hopes, wired dreams. The picture is labelled *Louise. Thirteen. Trials.* Wonder what she tried for, if she kept trying, why.

Kiss your wife's neck tonight at the stove. Take the pan from her hands. Touch that photograph, swirl it in your pocket. Keep twirling. Twirl for your life.

Interrogating the Kiss

How do you feel about baby birds gaping to be fed, the flayed beak?
Do you think this has anything to do with you? Why not?

How well do you know the kiss who broke out of my house? That one
kiss that swung off the moon and set a hundred others loose.

Have you ever whispered you'll cut me if I don't set you free?
When did you give a crowbar to your friends locked in my ribs? Why?

How do you feel about being compared to a red dress? When did you start
wearing leather? It's dangerous out there, haven't you heard?

Have you read the instructions stitched to your underwear? *Handle with care.*
Burn after use. Can you spell? Spell frenulum. Spell vulva. Radius. Ulna.

Now do it again. Is there anything to be learnt from paintings? Klimt, Magritte.
Do you identify with a gold leaf of autumn mornings, or a draped sheet?

When did you make my mouth a portrait gallery of people I no longer know?
Is it true you're tattooed with the numbers of all my missed calls?

Why did the kiss cross the road? A) To get, to get, to get, B) Because it could,
C) Because a kiss is born to rise on maroon wings and must fly to its death.

A kiss is a prayer that has forgot the words. A kiss is a girl kicking off
Mary-Janes and rolling in dirt to rub soap off her neck. Discuss.

The language of the kiss is dying, scientists say we've forgot. So why do you
speak only amongst yourself, knock on air? How is it to be glitter in a storm?

Note: 'a kiss is a red dress' is a line by Kim Addonizio.

In Praise of Disney Villains who Refuse to Retire

This is for the women who disguise a frown with flames,
the dusk of your eyelids and opera of fingertips
constructing scarlet cathedrals and knocking them down.

It's for mothering that rook on your shoulder,
a praise for crows' feet and your mirror of hecklers,
the hours of boiling unrequited love into lipstick and mist.

It's for your pageant of age, strapping a crown over horns.
This is for peeling a lonely night off the window, wearing
its cloak, ripping your spleen to kibble left for wolves.

It's for your disgrace, putting on that black dress, letting it
flow like a dozen bridesmaids holding off night.
If age is just a number, this is for calling it in the small hours

and breathing *fuck me* in its ear. It's for dancing
with lightning, stumbles, showing us a cane can conduct skies.

Here's to you, for making purple a sports car and sharing
the map to let us go roaring into our dawn.

Girls Who Shit in the Woods

It's more difficult than it looks to take those steps
through the woods. Side-stepping ditches, the bodies
Mother placed there embroidered with your face.
Crows dismembering silence, flicking burnt parts
across trees. The kid next-door's Girls Don't Poop T-shirt
winding around your ankles, and the Lord
peeping through thistles. He's always with us,
softly snipered under knitted toilet-roll dollies. Adrift
on an airbed in the ocean where you still don't know
why with the sun on your face, parents pink dots
arguing about the cost of whale-spotting trips,
something slipped out like an animal coming home.
Innocent as fish food, you pictured sated shrimp,
an iridescence of plankton born of your gracelessness,
a light show. But truth is, nature has never called
without you looking both ways, closing a blind, making alibis.
Long candlelit baths, facemasks, an inexplicable desire
to clean the bathroom at 11pm, shower running
over the sound of your drop in the water, a man
who calls your morning-breath kitten mouth
in the next room peeling rose petals off his back.
And yet you lower to pinecones, Snow White
penguined by jeans, leaves baring skeletons at your feet.
Long muscles somehow holding you upright.
Beneath branches what remains of the day fractured
into small pieces, you look up and relieve yourself,
a bird indifferently planting wild cherry. The wind
lifting into the world's whisper, yes, God is here.

Assessment for Snow Globe Addiction

Do you remember
who gave you that first holiday
you didn't attend? When your breath
became a burning warehouse, smoke blown
through Las Vegas? How often you've pelted
sweet wrappers at wedding dresses? When one
snow globe ballooned into ten, fifty, paned the walls
in bad bubble wrap? Have you stopped and woke up
shaking, itchy for snow globes? Looked through goggles
at small women on benches feeding birds, snow dyeing
crows into doves at the flip of a wrist? Do you worry
about water turning into varnish? Clarity tallowed,
a spaceman blinded by smoking in his helmet?
Are your fingertips smog, razing hurricanes
on beaches, plastic men under palm trees
showered in shrapnel? Are there
incidental bombs in your hands?
Have you ever said sorry to glass?
Given courtrooms party poppers?
Sprinkled the view of the Overlook Hotel
over friends sipping latte in cute cafés? Do you write
shopping lists and discover all you've written is Smash?
How long can you stare at the gap, bubbles in liquid
a slant spirit level? Do you drink glitter? Carry the globe
everywhere and picture dropping it? That shiny woman
like a flopping fish, unsure how to use all this air.

The Snowwoman Ponders Existence

if   i see the stars   throw   their   flowers at my coals
does someone's fire   glow   less   bright   tonight?
if i burn   ungloved hands   scarlet, bite   toes
is there   a   flame   inside me somewhere? was it   always
here? or   lit by the last   raspberry   licked by wind.
drawn from hot   mouths   skywriting   in   smoke?
why is the grass littered   in body   parts? how
can   i stand   surrounded by women not lucky   enough
to be   picked off   the   ground? why do people
roll   in   dazzling   bones
the   blood of my kind   carpeting the   land?
are the angels   swept   at   my feet sad they can't fly
but   must lay on   their back   facing the   shadow
of   swans? is   all   waving a   goodbye?
is everything   skin?   i've seen it   shovelled, arms,
breasts   moulded & flung, so why can't   i blink?
why can i   smell the   hunger of   rabbits?
how has my   unshaped heart   become a   map
for   animal lives: bird   hare   fox?
if   sunlight is my kryptonite. why do i wear
it sexy? make   jewellery of the   colours I bury?
how   do i go without   weeping but   make
it   look like a curtsy, lashes of my babies falling
latched onto fat   winter coats? where   do I end
& the hills   begin?   the   snowdrops
the   gulley   the   rain

Dysregulation as Snow Woman Word Search

1. Looking at a flaming building or at starbursts in a gym
2. A wonder if there's a place without slushies, fire trucks, bombs
3. Someone removing their fingers from across my eyes at night
4. What I want him to do to me, what other people have done
5. The daffodils finally opening the day of her funeral
6. A failed collage snipped from lipstick advertorials
7. The sensation of being a middle-aged woman painting
   at sunset recalling the strange sex of her youth
8. Clenched teeth in the Job Centre, putting on leopard skin
   and going out dancing with next week's gas money
9. Naked, dusting on talc, the flit of bird across the window
10. Studying infinite glove boxes as a car pulls away
11. Stretching alone in luminous morning, still the thought of a cat
12. The attempt to understand popular reactions to *Titantic*
13. The sweet sixteen goldish watch colouring a wrist green
14. Discovering a whisker in a place someone once licked
15. Another way you can leave, the ghosts of skin on a bathtub
16. Overnight snow, the last rosebud gnawed to a stub
17. The perpetual study of grass and incidental formations of land
    or a poetic image pushing into an hour where it has no business.

Answers in No Particular Order:

Flowers bright bite, blood angels must lay, women ground dazzling, mouths littered, surrounded, a less scarlet somewhere stars fire ungloved, I see someone's burn, seen it, so why hunger heart bird? Licked in parts, raspberry sky writing in body, without a cursty winter begin, do look at hills, my animal sunlight, throw glow hands inside me, smell the unshaped lives, my swept on swans skin, why the weeping, I go like fat, become hare, fly shadow goodbye.

The Afterlife of Girls

They stand behind us waiting for our footsteps
to slide open doors, the girls we once were.
Without a wave they drift off in the mall.
The Barbies they dressed as nuns are life-sized
ushers pointing at billboards flashing.
It's not their fault they couldn't fix us.
Who could? We got used to itchy hands
stroking Moomins and pencils in gift-shops.
They made us long for the sweet and the useless.
Sugar mice, vampire fangs, glitter. Often,
we were puppets, the girls we tried not to be
ran the show. They played pong in our chest,
bounced laughter through mouths that knew better,
peeled the years off our throats. Surprising,
how close they always were, collecting feathers,
guiding fingers to doodle bunny ears on politicians.
They crashed all appointments, coloured our cheeks
scarlet. Cost us. Still, it shocks us to see them go,
so late and so soon. A fog of gum, animal facts
and jingles winding between giant TVs.
At any point, we know the girls we once were can flop
on a beanbag, flick and see what we're doing now,
the women we'll be. But, of course, they don't.

The Probability of Summer

There are 4 boys and 2 girls at the dairy. What are the chances of sex? The boys take any work they get. 1 has witnessed the birth of a lamb. He has spoken about this 1.5 times. The same amount another has done it.

2 of the boys could be called men. Their jaws are fields after the hay has been baled. Their eyes are the same. 1 never speaks. Once, a horse licked his fingers on a frosty morning and he thought about death.

The average male thinks of sex 34 times a day. The average woman 18.6, according to *Psychologies*. No one subscribes to that here. There are 15 flavours of ice-cream the girls scoop in aprons.

1 was called a heifer when she was 6. The other sings pouring milk into the machine, July harvesting salt from her brow. 1 has a father who calls her Sweetheart. What difference does this make?

Both will empty the bins. Tourists licking cones, the boys eating lunch at picnic tables. 2 bring fruit, 1 a plastic pot of yesterdays. How many jokes must be told until someone feels like getting naked?

What is it like to be attractive and not care? Deduct that girl, she laughs easy, her eyes are stars that have already been wished on. It's the other a boy holds the dumpster open for like a chauffeur.

What is the likelihood of offering a lift after closing? What is she thinking getting in his car? How far can they drive? There are 101 sentences that can be interpreted as 'kiss me.' Which work?

The average cow makes 40,000 jaw movements a day. The girl hears dozing cattle while the boy speaks. What can he say she hasn't already heard? How long must some girl and some guy listen until they become someone?

The Penultimate Girl

I find myself in a forest, not the final girl but almost.
The one who's a virgin, and isn't, my promise ring
given to a pencil. The killer is out there, chainsaw
teething on the moon, stopping to sculpt
topiary animals en route. Maybe. There's a lot
of stopping and starting, roar/stutter, body parts.
I run, a gash on my forehead bleeding raspberry syrup,
my pet cushion brutally massacred, my underwear
hung in a tree as a prayer flag. I shouldn't have got caught
drawing pornography on misty windows. Or worn
lace stockings and wellies under a trench coat
to seduce men who like asparagus, stood outside
wildlife parks holding a boom-box high enough
to scare sparrows, had a meaningful relationship
with a knot of pine on a kitchen table or fallen in love
with a lemur with one eye. That killer is out there
buzzing closer. And I'm stumbling, throwing stars
of frost in my fist, lighting flamethrowers
of crocosmia, foxglove sword raised. A limo
of moonlight pulling up outside my house with daisies.
I climb in, sail the cutting room floor.

Poetry Club

While you are sleeping, every night, I slip out to the garage to let a poet punch me in the face. The moon is a boxing ring, reeks of lilies, chardonnay and blood. Those pearls you sweep up every morning aren't pearls.

I weave through the ropes, back to the pillow strapped to the workbench. I place a gumshield in my mouth. It looks identical to my work smile.

There's always a poet already there, staring me out, lacing metaphors to a wrist. *One. Two.* The bell pings. I jab and dance, knuckles cracking the frost of Emily Dickinson's ribs. I lash out, slice my fingers on the sharp fish of Elizabeth Bishop's mouth.

I stagger, socked by an observation of pine trees by a sea wall, that sunshine arrowed brick. Swilling defeat around my mouth, I stand and sway. Defeat tastes like spearmint gum, since you ask.

It doesn't come the way you'd think, losing. It never hits square-on, it takes years. Steals in bit by bit, a slow dawn sketching my room: a window, a bedpost, a plum bruised by the lip of the bowl. I hear air ring and stroke my cheek, the welt swollen as a gazed cloud, the ache in my ribs placed inside me with a bird.

Some days I open the curtains and the sun knocks me out, a poem in its fist. I look out, lick a split lip, so much autumn inside me, more reds than words.

Thanks & Acknowledgements

I would dearly like to thank Jane Commane for her encouragement and taking a chance on me, Jo Bell for her December lockdown prompts which woke me up, as well as the poets who kindly commented in group. I am grateful.

I'd like to thank The Poetry School who kindly awarded me a bursary for a course, and Victoria Kennefick for her enthusiasm and encouragement. I'd also like to thank Wendy Pratt for the Solstice course which brought me a snow woman.

I'd also like to give deepest thanks to Kate Fox for her work in autism, without which these poems would still be sitting in my drawer.

Last, but not least, I'd like to thank the journals and editors who published earlier drafts of some of the poems. I'm honoured to have been given space I've struggled for so long to believe I deserve. Thank you.

'Bunny Girls' (*I am Not a Silent Poet*). 'Girly' (I'll Show You Mine Sex Writing Competition). 'Miss Monroe's Body Double on *Something's Got to Give*' (*The Blacklight Engine Room*). 'The Usherette's Eczema', 'Psalm for a Street Swept by Plague' (*Butcher's Dog*). 'Curator of Rain' (as 'Slug Smackdown'), 'Hush', 'The Arrival of the Siberian Swan', 'The Blow Torch' (*The Lake*). 'Peat' (*Adhoc* Fiction site). 'Angel Mechanics' (Carmen Marcus' blog). 'Procedures for the Detective after Thelma & Louise' (*Mookychick*). 'Another Miss Universe' (*Deranged Women* anthology). 'Man Dusting', 'The Probability of Summer' (*Under the Radar*). 'The Survivalist's Guide to Love' (*Ink, Sweat & Tears*). 'In Praise of Disney Villains Who Refuse to Retire' (*Atrium Poetry*). 'The Still of Churches' (commended as 'Just a Deer' in the Manchester Cathedral Competition). '10:58am in November' (*Spelt* magazine).